AND BABY
MAKES SEVEN
BY PAULA VOGEL

★

★

DRAMATISTS
PLAY SERVICE
INC.

AND BABY MAKES SEVEN
Copyright © 1984, 1993, Paula Vogel

All Rights Reserved

SPECIAL NOTE

for David

AND BABY MAKES SEVEN was originally produced by Theatre with Teeth at the Eighteenth Street Playhouse, in New York City, opening in January, 1984. It was directed by Paula Vogel; the cast was as follows:

PETER .... Ted Montague
RUTH .... Sondra Allen
ANNA .... Cary Bickley

AND BABY MAKES SEVEN was produced at Theatre Rhinoceros in San Francisco, California, opening in February, 1986. It was directed by Kris Gannon; the set design was by Vola Ruben; the costume design was by Ann Marie Leimer; and the lighting design was by Cayenne Wood. The cast was as follows:

PETER .... Michael DeMartini
RUTH .... Sandra Langsner
ANNA .... Karen Lynn Seaton

AND BABY MAKES SEVEN was produced by Circle Repertory Company (Tanya Berezin, Artistic Director) at the Lucille Lortel Theatre in New York City, opening in May 1993. It was directed by Calvin Skaggs; the set design was by Derek McLane; the costume design was by Walker Hicklin; and the lighting design was by Peter Kaczorowski. The cast was as follows:

PETER .... Peter Frechette
RUTH .... Mary Mara
ANNA .... Cherry Jones

CHARACTERS

PETER LEVEN: Has the appearance of a precocious child.

RUTH ABRAMS: Short, dark and intense.

ANNA EPSTEIN: A little overweight right now.

THE CHILDREN

CECIL BARTHOLOMEW: Age 9, genius IQ. Played by Anna.

HENRI DUMONT: Age 8, French accent. Played by Ruth.

ORPHAN McDERMOTT: Age 7, with a stutter. Played by Ruth.

PLACE

A loft apartment in New York City. A window, which leads onto a fire escape.

TIME

The play takes place in the present.

AND BABY MAKES SEVEN

PROLOGUE TO ACT ONE

*In the darkness, we hear three children talking in their beds.
There is a glow from a clown nightlight.*

HENRI. And so that is how babies come to be made.

CECIL. Oh, God.

HENRI. Well, it is!

CECIL. You've got it all wrong, Henri.

HENRI. No, I do not. Do I, Orphanne?

ORPHAN. I-I-I d-d-don't kn-know.

HENRI. Well, Cecil, if you're so smart, how do you think babies
are made?

CECIL. Well, it's actually a complicated, sophisticated process. A
marvel of human technology.

ORPHAN. Umm-hmm.

CECIL. The process starts with intercourse between two humans
— a male and a female.

HENRI. Get to the good part. *(Laughs raucously.)*

CECIL. The male inserts his erect member into the female's vagina
and then begins to … uh, oscillate the member with increasing
rapidity until the … uh, friction causes orgasm.

HENRI. Oh, barf.

CECIL. At orgasm, thousands of millions of sperm are released
and swim their way upstream to the egg. Only one survives. It's
kind of a microcosm of Wall Street.

HENRI. This is boring.

CECIL. This is science. The sperm fertilizes the egg, which
becomes a fetus, which becomes a baby, until finally, the female
goes into contractions —

HENRI. Wait a minute, Cecil. Are you telling us that the baby

7

comes out of the lady's wee-wee hole?

CECIL. It's not a wee-wee hole. It's a vagina.

HENRI. Do you expect us to believe this?

CECIL. It's the truth!

HENRI. Orphanne? What do you vote for?

ORPHAN. I vote for th-the eggplant.

HENRI. Okay. That makes two votes for the eggplant. You're wrong, Cecil.

CECIL. You can't vote down the truth!

HENRI. Yes, we can ... This is a democracy. Maybe you came from a wee-wee hole. We came from the eggplant.

ORPHAN. W-w-wee-wee! *(Henri and Orphan begin to laugh.)*

HENRI. Cecil's a wee-wee head! *(Henri and Orphan erupt in laughter again.)*

CECIL. Stop it!!! Stop it!!! Or I'll make you stop!!!

HENRI. Wee-wee head!!! *(The kids continue to laugh. Suddenly, a door stage right cracks open in a stream of light. We see the figure of Peter, who closes the door behind him.)*

PETER. All right, boys. What's going on?

HENRI. Cecil's a wee-wee head!

PETER. Henri. Orphan. Settle down. It's time to go to sleep.

CECIL. Uncle Peter! Tell them! Make them stop! Tell them!

PETER. Tell them what, Cecil?

CECIL. How babies are made.

PETER. Oh. Well, uh, I think that's something you should discuss with Anna.

HENRI. Uncle Peter, Cecil used the v-word.

PETER. The v-word?

HENRI. For a lady's — you know.

CECIL. Vagina. Vagina. It's not a dirty word. It's clinical.

HENRI. That makes you a vagina-head. *(Henri and Orphan erupt again.)*

CECIL. Uncle Peter! Tell them! Please! Man to man!

ORPHAN. M-m-man t-t-to m-man! Mmm-hmm.

PETER. If I tell you how, will you boys settle down and go to sleep?

HENRI. All right. Just make it good ...

PETER. All right. It's your bedtime story. Okay? Well, when a man —

HENRI. Sit on my bed, please, Uncle Peter!!!

PETER. All right. *(Pause.)* Now, then, babies are made when a

8

man — Hey! Henri!!! What are you doing! Stop that!!!

HENRI. I'm just hugging you.

PETER. Well, don't hug me there! Now then, when a man and a woman really, really love one another, they decide to make a baby to share that love —

CECIL. Oh, brother. Just tell it straight, will you, Uncle Peter?

PETER. Okay. A man rams his hot throbbing member into a woman and humps so hard that he explodes just as she's screaming: "Don't stop, don't stop!" — Is that straight enough for you? *(Pause.)*

CECIL. Uncle Peter … you're not a well man. *(Pause.)*

HENRI. Uncle Peter?

PETER. Yes, Henri? What is it?

HENRI. I want to have your baby!!! *(Nursery music tinkles as lights fade up to Scene 1.)*

ACT ONE

Scene 1

Day One. A.M. The kitchen. Peter, Anna and Ruth sit around the table. They are in the middle of a discussion.

PETER. I think they have to go. That's all I'm saying!

RUTH. Look, Peter, you just waltz in here —

PETER. What's with the "waltz!" I've been here for a solid six months now —

RUTH. The boys have been here for a long, long time! And they'll be here for a long, long time to come —

ANNA. Honey, we should just hear Peter out —

RUTH. Peter — if they go, I go!

PETER. Look, this is nothing to get emotional about.

RUTH. This is something between Anna and me.

PETER. Not anymore it's not. We entered into a contract; now the three of us have equal say in the bringing up of our child.

ANNA. Honey — Peter doesn't think we're ... well, that the way we talk to our children is healthy.

PETER. Imaginary children.

RUTH. What do you mean, not "healthy"?

PETER. I've just noticed that you're both doing it a lot more. Going into character. Now whenever I'm around those ... "kids" are always with us.

RUTH. Well, Peter, you're one of the family now. Isn't that right, Anna?

ANNA. Honey — I think Peter has a point. We are doing the kids more often. All the time now.

PETER. Yes — it's become an obsession.

RUTH. I wouldn't call it that.

PETER. But you're doing it all the time!

RUTH. So what!!! And it's not all the time. It's just a way of releasing anxieties ...

PETER. Don't you think it would be better to address those anxieties directly?

RUTH. What the hell are you paying a hundred dollars an hour for?

PETER. I pay someone to listen to me. I don't go around talking to myself in a high tiny voice ... Cecil, the child genius. Henri, from that movie —

RUTH. *The Red Balloon* —

PETER. Whatever it was. And on top of it all, this wild child raised by a pack of dogs. I say they have to go.

RUTH/HENRI. And I say to you — you — you are a big, fat wee-wee head!

PETER. *(To Anna.)* You see? That's just the kind of thing I'm talking about.

ANNA. Look, the three of us have to work this out like mature, rational adults —

RUTH/HENRI. Wee-wee head!!!

ANNA. Ruth. Please. *(Shifts her weight.)* Ow. Damn. I don't believe it. I have to go to the bathroom. Again. *(Anna gets up heavily to her feet; she is very pregnant. She exits. Pause.)*

PETER. We have to remember that she's peeing for two now. *(Suddenly Ruth becomes Henri again.)*

RUTH/HENRI. *(With great significance.)* Uncle Peter? I loved the bedtime story you told me last night. You know.

PETER. Oh.

RUTH/HENRI. Will you tell us the same story ... tonight? And sit on my bed?

PETER. Ruth, I'm really not in the mood right now to play —

RUTH/HENRI. Can I sit in your lap?

PETER. Well, I'd really rather that you wouldn't — *(Ruth/Henri sits in Peter's lap, wriggling suggestively.)* What in the hell are you doing?

RUTH/HENRI. I'm finding a comfortable spot. *(Henri laughs.)* It's so lumpy, Uncle Peter.

PETER. Ruth — get up —

RUTH/HENRI. But, Uncle Peter, don't you like little boys?

PETER. Well, of course I — no! Not like that — come on, get up, Henri —

RUTH/HENRI. But first you have to ... give me something ... *(Anna comes into the room and sees Ruth in Peter's lap. As soon as Ruth sees Anna, she jumps up as Henri and throws her arms around Anna.)* Anniah!

ANNA. Henri!!! What were you doing to Uncle Peter?

11

RUTH/HENRI. Nothing.

ANNA. Were you bothering him again?

RUTH/HENRI. No. I didn't do nothing!

ANNA. Petey? Was Henri ... bothering you again? *(Henri appeals to Peter silently.)*

PETER. Ah ... no.

ANNA. Okay. Because you know, Henri, that we had that talk about no g-r-o-p-i-n-g. Remember? Not even if Uncle Peter wants you to.

RUTH/HENRI. I would like to go to my room, please!

PETER. By all means, be our guest. *(Ruth makes sounds of an offended Henri leaving the room, and slamming the door. Pause. Anna sits. Pause.)* Look, maybe it's me ... But I just think that the ... the line between reality and you know ... well, it's getting dangerously thin around here.

RUTH. We never do it out of the house. You know that.

PETER. That's not the point. What about when the baby comes? What kind of effect is it going to have on Emma or Nathan —

RUTH. What do you mean, Emma or Nathan? We haven't decided that yet. It might be Sigourney or Christopher —

ANNA. Oh, please, not this again. I don't give a damn what it's called. Just let it come out healthy.

RUTH/ORPHAN. I-I l-l-like th-the name Lassie.

ANNA. Yes, Orphan. That's a sweet name. But that's a name for a dog, honey.

RUTH/ORPHAN. *(Cooing agreement.)* Mmm-hmm.

ANNA. You want to name your baby sister in honor of the stray dogs of Port Authority who found you and took care of you?

RUTH/ORPHAN. *(Again, cooing.)* Mmm-hmm.

ANNA. Yes, sweetie, but we're bringing up the baby differently than you were. Remember when we found you behind a Greyhound bus last winter? Running on all fours and scratching with your hind legs? Well, your sister's going to have a much different upbringing than the dogs gave you.

PETER. That's for sure. No fleas for little baby Emma. Or Nathan. *(Suddenly Ruth/Orphan leans over and bites Peter savagely.)* Ow!!! Goddamn! —

ANNA. Orphan, no!!! Bad boy!!! You don't bite people! Now go to your room!!!

PETER. Look at that! The skin is practically broken! Now they're biting me!!!

RUTH. A flesh wound.

PETER. You bit me!

RUTH. Not me. Orphan. He's never going to break that habit.

PETER. I'm sitting here, bitten, and nobody cares! I'm trying to have a talk! I'm trying to take my responsibility seriously, like a grown man, and you two are —

ANNA/CECIL. Listen, Uncle Peter, calm down. You have to understand that you're hyperventilating from a very common syndrome.

PETER. Oh, Jesus. Now I get counseling from a nine-year-old doctoral candidate —

ANNA/CECIL. Okay, buddy. But I'm here. I just want you to know that. When you're having problems coping with those feelings of ... of being extraneous in the face of —

ANNA/RUTH. Woman creating —

PETER. Shut the fuck up!!! *(There is silence.)*

ANNA/CECIL. Golly.

RUTH. Cecil, why don't you go join your other brothers in the other room? I think "Sesame Street" is on.

CECIL. Do you think I'm a child? *(Noises of a wounded Cecil leaving the room. Pause.)*

ANNA. Petey? Do you want to talk?

PETER. No! No ... I've got to get out.

RUTH. Oh, come on, Peter. We were only playing around —

PETER. I've got to go. I'm late. I'll ... I'll see you later. *(Peter storms out of the room. Pause. The women look at each other.)*

RUTH. He's got to learn how to relax.

Scene 2

Day One. Late that night. Anna sits at the table playing solitaire. There is a key in the door, and Peter enters, very softly, so as not to wake the women.

ANNA. Peter? *(Peter jumps. Looks very sheepish and somewhat guilty.)*

PETER. Oh ... Hi. *(Pause.)* You didn't have to wait up, you know.

ANNA. I didn't. Ruthie got worried when you didn't show for dinner.

PETER. Oh. Ah — I ate out.

ANNA. *(Looking at him carefully.)* Uh-huh. *(Laughs.)* I'll bet you did. Did you have a good time with the boys? *(Peter becomes beet red.)*

PETER. Umm ... well, not a bad time, you know ...

ANNA. Promise me you're being careful ...

PETER. I'm being so careful.

ANNA. How's your wound? — Are you still mad at us?

PETER. I wasn't mad. Just ... just concerned.

ANNA. It's all going to work out fine.

PETER. I ... have my doubts sometimes.

ANNA. Why?

PETER. Well, sometimes, with you and Ruth ... I feel like I'm in the way.

ANNA. That's nonsense. We don't feel that way.

PETER. Maybe we made a mistake ... threesomes never work.

ANNA. Now is not the time to get cold feet. You've been saying since college that you wanted to have a child ...

PETER. I know, but —

ANNA. *(In an intimate way.)* Wasn't it fun?

PETER. It was pretty funny, too.

ANNA. Oh, but also romantic. No turkey baster for little Emma. The bottle of champagne from Ruth, that little inn —

PETER. The innkeeper thinking we were newlyweds —

ANNA. Our little plots ... The Nubian boy spread on a Persian rug, the English schoolboy being disciplined — which was your favorite?

PETER. Well, personally I liked the one you told me about the young Greek sailor, swabbing the deck on his knees in the hot Mediterranean sun ...

ANNA. Oh, yes, that one was good, too. *(Pause.)*

PETER. Anna? I just wanted you to know ... that the fantasies weren't ... necessary.

ANNA. Oh, Petey. How sweet.

PETER. *(Shyly.)* I just wanted you to know ... I really miss breasts.

ANNA. Really? That must be awful ... *(Anna looks down and strokes her breast.)*

PETER. It's so alien to me. That softness ...

ANNA. Well, you know, Petey, whenever you get hit by the urge, you can always feel one ...

PETER. Can I?

ANNA. Of course you can. Be my guest. Go ahead, it won't bite you ... *(Peter hesitantly puts out his hand to stroke Anna's breast. Ruth, still half-asleep, enters in her pajamas.)*

RUTH. Petey? Are you home? You okay?

PETER. Yes. *(He starts to remove his hand, but Anna holds it to her breast.)*

RUTH. What are you two up to?

PETER. I'm, um, stroking Anna's breast.

RUTH. *(Totally unconcerned.)* Oh. That's nice.

ANNA. There's room for one more here.

RUTH. *(Enthused.)* Okay. *(Ruth goes to Anna's other side and gently puts her hand on Anna's breast. Peter and Ruth look at each other. Ruth smiles. Anna smiles, and sighs.)*

ANNA. Ahhh.

Scene 3

Day Two. Ruth and Peter in the kitchen. On the table is a large rubber tub filled with water, towels, a baby bottle, diapers and a life-sized doll. Ruth holds a baby-care book, from which she reads.

RUTH. Ready? *(Peter is rolling up his sleeves, and looking grim.)*

PETER. Let's go.

RUTH. Where do you want me to start from?

PETER. The beginning of the book!

RUTH. Okay. *(Reads.)* "Parenthood is many things to many people — a new beginning, a new definition of self, a challenge and a — "

PETER. *(Irritably.)* Oh, skip that crap!

RUTH. You said from the beginning. *(Pause.)* You know, Petey, is this really necessary? When the baby comes home —

PETER. I asked you to help me!

RUTH. I'm helping, I'm helping ... I just don't think parenthood is something you bone up on from a book — *(Peter gives her a look.)* Okay. *(Flips through the index.)* How about starting with ... let's see — "Positions, comma, proper, comma, for carrying newborns"?

PETER. All right. Now we're cooking with gas.

RUTH. Okay. Do you have Junior? Right. Page nineteen. *(Peter picks up the doll.)* "It is important to carry the baby so that its neck is always supported. Do not touch the soft spot at the top of the

15

baby's head, and hold it in such a fashion so that your hand supports the weight of the head." *(Peter tries to accomplish this, leaving the body dangling at a strange angle.)*

PETER. Shit. That's not right.

RUTH. *(Trying to continue with a straight face.)* "One hand should cushion the back of the baby's head and the thumb and wrist of the adult will provide a bulwark for the infant's neck ... "

PETER. Christ! Can't they write these things in plain English? Here — take this — let me see that book! *(Peter thrusts the doll at Ruth, while grabbing the book. Ruth tenderly takes the doll, demonstrates perfect carrying position and smiles at Peter.)*

RUTH. You're at a disadvantage. You never played with dolls.

PETER. Says you.

RUTH. Hold this thing. *(Thrusts the doll at Peter.)* The right way. *(Peter holds the plastic doll like a pro.)* That's great, Peter!

PETER. You really think so?

RUTH. The Madonna herself couldn't do better.

PETER. *(Pleased; with renewed confidence.)* Okay. Hit me with the hard stuff. *(Ruth flips to the back of the book again.)*

RUTH. Okay. "Bathing, comma, newborns."

PETER. I'm ready.

RUTH. Well, take its little tutu off first.

PETER. Oh. Right.

RUTH. Now then. "Nothing can be more slippery and capricious to hold than the newborn infant, soapy and wriggling like an eel on the proverbial hook — " *(Stops.)* What moron wrote this?

PETER. Come on.

RUTH. "The first bath is every parent's nightmare. To avoid tragic consequences — " blah-dy, blah-dy, blah ... "Carefully lower the child into the water, with one hand supporting the child's — " blah, blah, blah. "With the other hand, wet the child's — " blah, blah, blah ... Now comes the tricky part.

PETER. It's all a matter of concentration.

RUTH. *(With increased sadism.)* "When removing the baby from the bath water, have a towel ready to wrap the infant's tiny body so that the child will not slip from your grasp, and possibly injure its delicate, tissue-thin membranes ... " *(Peter begins to slip with the doll. We see him frantically grasp its little plastic parts, to no avail. The doll eludes his hold, and crashes into the tub.)*

PETER. AHH — AHH — Goddamn!!! *(Beat. Ruth and Peter watch the doll float. They try to control themselves, but erupt in laughter. Peter holds the doll's face underwater, then tosses the doll into the air.)* Thirsty? Glub, glub, glub, glub, glub ... Good baby! Daddy's baby! Baby go boom? Don't touch the soft spot!!! Wheeee! Go to Ruthie — *(Peter tosses the doll to Ruth, who catches it. In a split second, we hear Henri's maniacal giggle. Then before Peter can respond, Ruth calls:)*

RUTH.   Hut one and Hut two! *(Peter and Ruth break out into football fantasy.)*

PETER.   *(Simultaneously with Ruth.)* Hike! He drops back to pass, he's forced out, out of the pocket, he's rolling to the right, reading the defense, now he's scrambling, it looks like he's going long! Yes! He's going to throw the bomb —

RUTH.   *(Simultaneously with Peter.)* Hike! She's splitting the defense, she's crossing into the flat, the crowd's going wild, can you hear that excite — she fakes a move to the corner — penalty for traveling! She's open and there's — *(Peter tosses the baby doll across the room at Ruth just as Anna enters and catches the doll in surprise. Calmly Anna moves downstage with the baby; the other two are embarrassed. With motherly care, Anna sets the baby down on the table.)*

Scene 4

Henri is in the kitchen, humming softly.

HENRI.   And now *pour le dejeuner.* A little *poisson?* Or *peut-etre —* a little *poulet — cordon bleu?* Or maybe steak Dijon? *(Stands in front of the refrigerator, contemplating the choices. He opens the refrigerator door and gasps in disgust.)* Peanut butter and jelly! Peanut butter and jelly! *Avec* Wonderbread!

RUTH.   *(Calls to the offstage Anna.)* Anna, you want a PBJ?

ANNA.   *(Offstage.)* No thanks. I'm going to take a nap. *(Ruth becomes Henri again. Henri sighs, then begins to work. He gathers the bread, peanut butter, jelly and knife on the table, arranges them. He looks at them. He takes out a nice plate and linen napkin, grabs a silk rose in a vase, and rearranges it all into a still life. Satisfied, he begins to create his sandwich, making a sensuous meal out of his peanut butter and jelly. As he works, he sings a medley of Maurice Chevalier hits. [Since it's really Ruth doing Henri imitating Maurice Chevalier, it's not as awful as the real thing.] He hums "Louise," occasionally substituting with "Henri.")*

HENRI. "Every little breeze seems to whisper 'Henri' — da dada da, da dada da — 'Henri' — da da da da — da da da da — 'I love you, love you — '" *(Henri modulates into "Mimi," changing lyrics freely for "Cecil." As Henri sings, he completes his sandwich, does a light soft-shoe with the plate, puts the plate back on the table. Then Henri dances from the room for a second. Ruth returns as Orphan, walks into the kitchen. Orphan sees the peanut butter sandwich; stops. Looks around, sees no one. Orphan goes to the table, and sniffs the sandwich. Orphan likes what he smells.)*

ORPHAN. Mmm-hmmm! *(Orphan takes a huge bite of the sandwich. Orphan stops, looks around, furtively leaves the room. Ruth returns as Henri, and comes sauntering back into the room still singing vintage Chevalier. Sees sandwich. Stops. In rage, picks it up and sees a big bite gone from its middle.)*

HENRI. WHO ... Who ... Who did this? What big, fat, humongous *couchon* did this to me? *(Henri/Ruth ducks under the kitchen table and waits. We see a hand sneak from under the edge of the table toward the sandwich, and hear:)*

ORPHAN. Ahhh-hhhah!!! *(Ruth/Orphan stands, takes the sandwich, smiles; and just as he's about to take a bite:)*

HENRI. All right, Orphanne! Hold it right there! That's my peanut butter sandwich!

ORPHAN. *(Snarl.)* NAA-NOOOOOOH! *(Orphan starts to eat. Orphan/Henri struggle with both of Ruth's hands.)*

HENRI. Put it down —

ORPHAN. *(Baring fangs.)* Sahh-sssahhh!!!

HENRI. I'm going to ... *(Henri makes bopping noises; Orphan starts to cry.)*

ORPHAN. GRR ... *(Orphan bites the air several times.)*

HENRI. OOWW! *(Henri starts to cry. Ruth's hand does a Dr. Strangelovian battle with her other hand, fighting for possession of the peanut butter and jelly. In the midst we hear her sing Wagner, etc. Finally, Ruth, as Orphan, pops the entire sandwich in her mouth in triumph.)*

ORPHAN. MMMM-MMMMMMMM!!! *(Ruth suddenly stops, with peanut butter crammed in her mouth, turning to see Anna watching her from the hallway. Ruth tries to manage a smile with her PBJ-smeared mouth.)*

Scene 5

In the morning. Anna sits at table, drinking coffee. Peter sits, smoking and brooding.

PETER. I feel bad about our fight the other day. But ...
ANNA. What fight?
PETER. About the kids.
ANNA. Oh, forget it. That wasn't a fight. That was a discussion. It's only a fight when something gets broken. *(Just then, there's a tremendous crash offstage. Anna does not blink. We hear Ruth, offstage, overlapping as Henri and Orphan.)*
HENRI. *(Offstage.)* Now look what you've done, Orphanne!
ORPHAN. *(Offstage.)* T-tough n-n-noogies. *(Offstage noise continues.)*
PETER. I ... I shouldn't have yelled at Cecil like that.
ANNA. Well, you know, Peter, he is imaginary —
PETER. Of course I know he's —
ANNA. Believe me, I know how easy it is to get confused about that sometimes, but at a time like this, you have to keep it separate —
PETER. I have to! ... That's what I'm trying to talk to you about! It's not my problem!
ANNA. Then why are you getting upset?
HENRI. *(Offstage.)* I get to wear that shirt! That's not yours, Orphanne!
ORPHAN. *(Offstage.)* N-now it is.
HENRI. *(Offstage.)* You take it off!
ORPHAN. *(Offstage.)* M-m-make m-me, Frog Boy.
PETER. It's very hard to talk around here sometimes.
HENRI. *(Offstage.)* Don't call me Frog Boy! *(Sounds of fighting.)*
ANNA. Look. I'm always ready to listen to your point of view, Peter ...
PETER. Okay, then, I just want to explain why I think we should stop — *(Sounds of Henri crying.)*
HENRI. *(Offstage.)* I AM GOING TO KILL YOU, ORPHANNE!
ANNA. Ah, excuse me, Peter — *(Anna gets up and crosses to the bedroom door. She stands there, with her back to us.)*
CECIL. Listen, you two. Will you please grow up? What is your

19

problem? *(Silence.)* Well, then, let Orphan wear that shirt today. Henri, you can wear my Fiorucci shirt with the fish —

HENRI. *(Offstage; delighted.)* All right! *(Anna returns to her seat. Beat.)*

ANNA. I'm sorry, Peter. You were saying?

PETER. Never mind.

ANNA. Oh, come on, Petey, don't be that way. *(Peter drinks his coffee.)*

PETER. What way?

ANNA. Can I have a sip of your coffee? Oh, come on. Do you think the kid's going to come out with a mushroom head if I have some caffeine?

PETER. Okay. I think mushrooms are cute.

ANNA. *(Swallowing.)* Oh my God —

PETER. Don't you have a doctor's appointment today?

ANNA. Tomorrow. At two. *(Ruth enters, in a Fiorucci fish shirt.)*

RUTH. Good morning, Petey.

PETER. Morning.

RUTH. What did I do?

ANNA. I think Peter wants to talk to us, honey.

RUTH. Okay. Talk, Peter. *(Peter takes a breath for patience and strength.)*

PETER. It's about the kids —

RUTH. Oh. Okay, you guys. I've made a decision.

ANNA. We're going to stop?

RUTH. Well ... not just like that.

PETER. I don't understand.

RUTH. Look, I want to get my last inch of fantasy out of them. I can't just stop doing them, just like that. I'll always be wondering: Will Cecil become a geophysicist? Will Henri go back to Paris? Will Orphan become fully socialized?

ANNA. So what are you proposing?

RUTH. We're going to tidy up the plots. No loose ends dangling. Starting tomorrow. We're going to kill them. One by one. First Orphan. Then Henri. Cecil will be the last to go. *(Anna and Peter stare at Ruth. Ruth smiles.)*

Scene 6

Afternoon. Ruth is loosely bound in a chair with kitchen nylon cord rope. She has a gag in her mouth. Anna enters from front door, carrying shopping bag. As she turns, Anna sees Ruth.

ANNA. Ruth!!! *(The shopping bag drops. Ruth casually removes the gag from her mouth with a free hand.)*

RUTH. Hi, honey. What'd the doctor have to say?

ANNA. What is all this!!! Are you all right? —

RUTH. I'm sorry, I just wanted to surprise you —

ANNA. Surprise me!!! Are you crazy? *(Anna stops, pants.)*

RUTH. I'm sorry. Close the door. Are you all right?

ANNA. Christ. You almost made me break my water. *(Anna sits.)*

RUTH. I'm sorry. It was stupid.

ANNA. What in the hell are you doing? Why are you bound and gagged?

RUTH. I'm not. Orphan is.

ANNA. Oh. I see.

RUTH. I'm afraid I have some bad news. About Orphan.

ANNA. You're pushing the envelope, Ruthie, you really are.

RUTH. Are you listening? He ... he went into a convulsion shortly after you left and I rushed him to St. Vincent's. Honey? You know how all these months, Orphan's been, well, stuttering? Biting? Having little fits?

ANNA. *(Starting to giggle.)* I don't believe this. Yes, yes, go on ...

RUTH. And ... and you know how hard it's been to get him to take a bath? Well — it's serious. Brace yourself. All this time he's had ... rabies. And we didn't know.

ANNA. Rabies!!!

RUTH. And now it's too late to do anything. He's in the last stages.

ANNA. I see.

RUTH. So the doctors let me bring him home.

ANNA. How much time does he have left? — Are we really going through with this?

RUTH. Yes. We are. He ... he doesn't have much time left. An hour or two.

ANNA. And they let him out?

RUTH. There's ... there's a shortage of beds.

ANNA. Uh-huh. *(Pause.)* Rabies simplex or rabies complex?

RUTH. Come on, you have to play along with this! Do you want to talk to Orphan?

ANNA. Is he lucid?

RUTH. Well, he goes in and out. Be careful. He might try to bite you.

ANNA. Okay. *(Ruth replaces the gag and sits in the chair as Orphan. Anna carefully takes off the gag, and Orphan almost bites her.)* Whew! That was a close one. Orphy? Baby? Can you hear me?

ORPHAN. Grrr-grr-sah, sah, t-t-t — the d-d-dogs, k-k-k-k — *(Makes strange little popping noises.)* Pop! Pop-pop-pop —

ANNA. Oh, God, Ruth, this is awful —

ORPHAN. M-m-m-milkkkkkk; w-warmm, w-warm mmmilk ... t-ttoo, t-too mmany others ... have to k-kick them away. T-to ggett the m-m-milkkk ... *(Orphan makes suckling noises.)*

ANNA. Oh, Jesus.

RUTH. He's coming 'round.

ORPHAN. Mmm-hmmm.

ANNA. Baby? Can you hear me?

ORPHAN. *(Cooing agreement.)* Mmm-hmmm.

ANNA. Oh, sweetie. Are you in pain?

ORPHAN. Nah-noh. N-no pain.

ANNA. *(Kneeling by Orphan and stroking his hair.)* Honey? How did this happen? Can you remember?

ORPHAN. Mmm-hm.

ANNA. Did you get bitten?

ORPHAN. I, I was pp-playing by Port Authority and these b-b-boys were th-throwing s-stones at th-this d-d-dog. And th-that made me mad. *(Pops his eyes for a second.)* So-so I, I called, "H-here, d-d-ddoggie." And it came to me.

ANNA. Was it walking funny?

ORPHAN. *(Sweetly.)* Mmm-hmmm.

ANNA. How?

ORPHAN. L-l-like a c-crab.

ANNA. Oh, God.

ORPHAN. *(Excited.)* A-and it had a b-b-beard. A wh-white b-b-beard. L-like Mr. B-b-bbubble!

ANNA. Yes, honey. Like your bubble bath, Mr. Bubble. Then what happened?

ORPHAN. I-I petteded the d-dog. B-because it reminded me … of … *(His voice goes strangely low.)* Mother.

ANNA. Ruthie. I can't go through with this. This is just too awful.

RUTH. We've got to go through with this. It's almost over.

ANNA. Well, hurry up, then!

RUTH. Okay. He's going into his last grand mal. Look out. Stand back. *(Orphan starts to make strange buzzing noises in his throat. When he erupts into speech, it should be reminiscent of the many voices of Mercedes McCambridge in* The Exorcist.*)*

ORPHAN. "Fuck Me, Jesus!" HEH HEH heh heh … zzzzzz. Scratch. ZZZZZ. Scratch. "A p-p-plague o-o-o' both your houses!!! — Z-z-zounds, a d-d-dog, a rrratt, a m-mouse, a k-k-k-kcat, to sccratch a m-man to death!!!" … "W-washed, I said. Are they washed? Arggh, that unwashed gggggrrr-grape has transported her soul." K!!! K!!! "Da-da-DAMIEN! W-w-why you d-do this to me?!" Pop!!! Pop!!! Poppoppoppoppp Put out the l-light, and t-then p-put out the l-light! Mmm-hmmm … "Sahh, sa-hhhh-Sunn … Mother, g-give me th-the sahh-sun." *(A small pause, then accelerated.)* Poppoppoppoppoppp "Pardon me b-boys; is th-that the Chchchatten-chatenn-Ch — " GRRR!!! … Woof, woof, woof. *(Bites the air three times.)* "Good night, ladies; good n-night, GooGooGooJoob!!! — O, UNTIMELY DEATH?!" *(Pause.)* Sit! Stay!!! … "Out, d-damned Spot!!!" *(Suddenly, Orphan looks up, quiet, alert. Hums the theme song from "Lassie." Listens; then in a plaintive high voice:)* "L-l-lassie c-come … hh-omme … " *(Orphan suddenly slumps over in his chair. Orphan is still. A pause.)*

ANNA. Orphan? Orphan!!! *(Ruth sits upright and takes off the gag and rope.)*

RUTH. *(Cheerfully.)* The end!!!

Scene 7

Cecil [Anna] and Henri [Ruth] hold a children's service for Orphan in the kitchen. They hold hands. Both are wearing black armbands. Cecil carries his bear, Sidney, who also wears an armband.

HENRI. *(Teary.)* So … so now what do we do, Cecil?

CECIL. *(Pale and dry-eyed.)* Well, I, uh, think it might be appropriate to the, uh, occasion if we sing Orphan's favorite song.

HENRI. Okay. *(The two sing in a sweet, high boy's soprano.)*
HENRI and CECIL.

    Had a dog and his name was Blue
    Had a dog and his name was Blue
    Had a dog and his name was Blue
    Betcha five dollars, he was a good 'un, too.
    Here, Blue:
    You good dog, you.

    Old Blue died and he died so hard
    Old Blue died and he died so hard
    Old Blue died and he died so hard
    Dug little holes all over my yard.

    Here, Blue:
    You good dog, you.
    Here, Blue:
    I'm a-comin' there too.

CECIL. Well, Orphan. I don't know if I think you're in heaven. I stopped believing in a divine presence when I was six, so there's really no way of knowing. But, uh, I do believe in the laws of physics. And that matter can't be destroyed, but only changed. So I know you're somewhere. And maybe you can hear me. And I just want to say, that, uh, I'll never forget you. You'll always be with me. *(Gently turns to Henri.)* Henri? Do you have something you want to say to Orphan?
HENRI. *(Quavering.)* Well, Orphanne, I just want to say that … *(Starts to break.)* … that when you wanted to eat my peanut butter and jelly sandwich, I'm sorry I didn't let you — *(Gives vent to heart-rendering cries on Cecil's shoulder.)* Oh, Cecilll …
CECIL. *(Comforting Henri ardently.)* I know. I know, Henri. It's all right. We have each other. *(Fiercely.)* I won't let anything happen to you. I swear it!

PROLOGUE TO ACT TWO

When the house lights have dimmed, we hear light snoring, sweet and melodious, as only an eight-year-old's can be. The clown nightlight is on.

GHOST OF ORPHAN. *(Ethereally.)* C-c-c-Ce-cillll ...
CECIL. Hh-huhnh? *(Henri's soft snoring is the only response.)* Henri? Did you say something? *(Henri whistles on.)* Guess not.
GHOST OF ORPHAN. C-C-CECILLL!!!
CECIL. *(Wide awake.)* Who ... who is that?!
GHOST OF ORPHAN. O-o-Orphan ... or a p-piece of him.
CECIL. O-o-Orphan? Oh, my God.
GHOST OF ORPHAN. L-list, l-list, O list! If thou didst ever thy d-dear brother l-love, revenge his f-foul and m-most un-un-un-n-n —
CECIL. Unnatural —
GHOST OF ORPHAN. Mm-hmm! ... M-murder.
CECIL. Murder? Murder?
GHOST OF ORPHAN. Mmm-hmm! M-murder m-most f-foul and m-most un-un-un-n-n —
CECIL. Unnatural —
GHOST OF ORPHAN. *Adieu! Adieu!* C-c-Cecil, remember me. Mmm-hmm!
CECIL. Wait!!! Orphan? — Wait! *(Pause. Then, urgent.)* Henri! Henri!
HENRI. Zzzz — What? What is it, Cecil? Cecil? You're ... you're shaking!
CECIL. It's just ... angst — Henri, we've got to get out of here.
HENRI. What? But why?
CECIL. Do you think ... what happened to Orphan ... was strange?
HENRI. *(Trembling.)* I ... don't know.
CECIL. I don't think what happened to Orphan happened ... by accident. I know it wasn't an accident.
HENRI. *(Starting to cry.)* How ... how do you know?
CECIL. I just know.

HENRI. Oh, Cecil — what are we going to do?

CECIL. We've got to get out of here.

HENRI. But where … where are we going to go?

CECIL. Listen. Henri, tomorrow I want you to act like nothing's different. I want you to pack a few things into the Channel Thirteen bag and hide it under the bed.

HENRI. Maybe we could sleep tonight with Uncle Peter!

CECIL. No. I don't think he can be trusted. I think Uncle Peter's one of them … We'll go to bed, and then when Anna and Ruth are sleeping, we'll slip on out of here.

HENRI. *(Crying.)* I don't think Anna and Ruth would really, really harm —

CECIL. They're not themselves. Ever since that baby.

HENRI. Yeah. I hate that baby.

CECIL. We've got to run away.

HENRI. Okay.

CECIL. Try to get some sleep. *(Henri cries softly; Cecil and Henri peer anxiously into the darkness as the lights fade up into Act Two.)*

ACT TWO

Scene 8

The next morning. Anna is making coffee. She wears a black armband. Peter sits at the table.

PETER. So what exactly happened?

ANNA. Well, he frothed, went into a frenzy and badly misquoted Shakespeare. Then he died.

PETER. How are the other two taking it?

ANNA. They're devastated. Henri turned down ice cream last night.

PETER. Poor lad.

ANNA. That's easy for you to say. *(Pause. Peter tries again.)*

PETER. So who's next? Henri or Cecil?

ANNA. Henri. It's my turn to bump him off. I want it to be painless. Orphan's demise was just too awful for me.

PETER. When's it gonna happen?

ANNA. Why? Want front-row seats?

PETER. I'm just asking, Anna. That's all.

ANNA. *(Trying to control her irritability.)* I know. I'm sorry. I just don't know.

PETER. Tonight?

ANNA. I don't know. I don't know. Don't rush me.

PETER. Sorry. *(Ruth enters, wearing a black armband and Peter's shirt.)*

RUTH. Morning, you guys. I gotta run.

ANNA. That's Peter's shirt.

PETER. Thought it looked familiar.

ANNA. Did you ask if you could wear it? *(Ruth and Peter look at each other. There is a moment of uneasy silence.)*

RUTH. *(Then, casually.)* Um, Petey, would you mind terribly, old man, if I borrowed your shirt?

PETER. Not at —

ANNA. *(Angry and starting to get loud.)* That's not the point! Jesus,

Ruthie, you can't just go around using other people's things without —
PETER. I really don't mind.
ANNA. But that's not the point!
RUTH. I asked him. Okay? I can't wear your things right now, they don't fit —
ANNA. There's gotta be some respect for other people's property around here.
RUTH. Sweetie, there's no reason to get —
ANNA. Don't fucking condescend to me! Like I'm the one who's crazy! It drives me nuts to hear the way you both talk to me, sometimes, like I'm a goddamn carton of eggs that has to be carried very carefully or —
PETER. *(Very calmly.)* We're not talking to you like that, Anna —
ANNA. Like hell you're not —
RUTH. What do you want from us?
ANNA. Just some respect! Some order in this household! Some quiet and some, some … You two just traipse in and out at all hours of the day while I sit here, bloated and tethered like some goddamn Goodyear blimp on Super Bowl day. I'm supposed to give up coffee, smoking, drinking, fucking, spicy foods, and I'm expected to be understanding of what Ruth wants, what Peter needs. Who the fuck am I, some kind of knocked-up Miss Manners? It's ninety degrees in August, and I can't get a seat on the subway! I fucking hate New York, and I just want to see my knees again! I WANT TO KILL, MAIM, MOON THE NEIGHBORS! *(Takes a breath; continues a bit more calmly.)* It would be nice, too, if Peter would pick his shoes up when he takes them off instead of leaving them in the middle of the floor for me to trip over, so I don't have to worry about dropping the goddamn baby in a burst of placental juice all over the —
RUTH. Maybe it would be a good idea if you went in and laid down. You're just having …
ANNA. I'm just what … What?
RUTH. You're having one … of … those —
ANNA. Don't say it!!! Don't you dare fucking say it! *(Smashes her coffee cup. She crosses to the bedroom, stops, and says with great dignity.)* You can both suck my imaginary dick! *(She exits. There is a moment of silence. Ruth picks up a shard of the coffee cup.)*
RUTH. I think we're having a fight.
ANNA. *(Offstage.)* AND DON'T YOU DARE TELL ME IT'S HORMONES! *(There is a crash offstage from the bedroom.)*

28

PETER. Maybe I should ... just pick up my shoes and leave the two of you alone for a while ... *(Peter stands; Ruth rounds on him.)*
RUTH. Don't start tippy-toeing out of here! *(Beat.)* For once, when the shit starts to fly, just ... just stay here, can't you? *(Peter takes a breath.)*
PETER. Okay. *(Ruth and Peter look around the room. Peter goes and picks up the various pairs of shoes and neatly arranges them under the table; Ruth, equally contrite, begins to pick up the shattered coffee mug and rinse the dishes. Peter straightens up magazines. Ruth picks up a few articles of clothing and takes them into the bathroom, while Peter waters the plants. They stop and look at the room, which is a bit more ordered. Then they sit at the table, tentatively smile at each other. Pause.)* So ... what are you going to do today?
RUTH. *(Quietly and miserably.)* Have a shitty day.
PETER. Sounds like fun. Can I join you?
RUTH. Listen, Peter — what are you doing this afternoon?
PETER. Nothing, I guess.
RUTH. There's something I want you to do for me.
PETER. Sure. What?
RUTH. Would you take Cecil and Henri to the zoo?
PETER. Me?
RUTH. It would cheer Ann — it would cheer them up. They're really upset. Would you?
PETER. Oh, Ruthie — do you really think we should be doing this outside the home?
RUTH. They won't be with us much longer. Please.
PETER. Well, they do need a strong male role model right now.

Scene 9

Day Four. The same. Peter, Henri and Cecil at the zoo. All three are wearing black armbands. Peter holds Henri and Cecil by the hand.

PETER. Look boys. The orangutans — they're always good for a laugh. *(Cecil and Henri watch, glumly. Then, Henri, excited, begins to laugh.)*

HENRI. Uncle Peter! Look!!! The monkey's pulling his pudding! In front of everybody! *(Henri laughs again.)*
PETER. Oh, Henri, you always think the worst — *(He looks. Then, hurriedly.)* — Ah, maybe we ought to go see the chimpanzees. Come on, Henri.
HENRI. But I want to watch the monkey pull — !
PETER. I said come on. *(Peter drags Henri over to the next cage, a few feet away.)* Look Cecil! The chimps!!! They're your favorites, aren't they?
CECIL. Yes.
PETER. They're awfully cute.
CECIL. Yes.
PETER. God. They look just like humans.
CECIL. *(Pensively begins to recite:)* "Never forget that every single organic being around us strives to increase in numbers; that each lives by a struggle at some period in its life; that heavy destruction inevitably falls either on the young or the old."
PETER. That's Darwin, isn't it? Come on, Ceepie, lighten up.
CECIL. "Thus, from war of nature, from famine and death, all organic beings advance by one general law — namely, multiply, vary, let the strongest live, and the weakest die ... " *(Cecil suddenly grips Peter and buries his head into Peter's side, weeping softly.)*
HENRI. Uncle Peter?
PETER. Yes, Henri?
HENRI. What's angst?
PETER. It's a kind of ... sadness. A German sadness.
HENRI. Is Cecil having angst?
PETER. Yes.
HENRI. Why?
PETER. Evolution. Come on, boys, let's go home.

Scene 10

Late at night. Anna and Henri.

HENRI. Is Uncle Peter in bed?
ANNA. Hello, baby. It's mighty late for you to be up, isn't it?

HENRI. I'm no longer a baby, Anniah. I have to talk to you — alone.

ANNA. Uh-huh. Is this about your allowance again?

HENRI. You would never, ever lie to me, would you? *(Anna immediately becomes guilty.)*

ANNA. Of course not. Why?

HENRI. Cecil has some strange ideas. I told him he was wrong, but still —

ANNA. What strange ideas?

HENRI. Cecil thinks that ... something terrible happened to Orphan. And that something terrible is going to happen to us. *(Anna averts her eyes.)*

ANNA. *(Trying to laugh.)* Where does Cecil get these ideas? I'll talk to him.

HENRI. No! Cecil must not know I have come to you. You would never let anything happen to me? Or to Cecil? Would you?

ANNA. Of course not! It's time for you to be in bed — *(Anna does not look Henri in the eyes.)*

HENRI. Why do you not look at me?

ANNA. *(Looks directly at Henri.)* I would never hurt you. You know that.

HENRI. I knew you would not. I knew Cecil was wrong. So we do not have to run away.

ANNA. Run away! You were going to run away?!

HENRI. But now we do not have to. And I don't have to tell Uncle Peter.

ANNA. Tell what to Uncle Peter?

HENRI. Oh, nothing. Nothing you would want Uncle Peter to know. And as long as Cecil and I are safe, then I know nothing.

ANNA. What's that supposed to mean?

HENRI. Peter still thinks he is the father to your child. You have led him to think so.

ANNA. He most certainly is! I should know. Why are you —

HENRI. I have reason to think otherwise. We both have reason to think otherwise.

ANNA. I don't know what you are talking about —

HENRI. You will hear me out. I have learned a lot in your country. I know how to count up to nine. In English.

ANNA. What are you implying?

HENRI. That I am the father to your child.

ANNA. Whoa. Time out, Ruthie. We agreed never to —

HENRI. It was late in November. All the leaves had fallen. Ruse was out of town. We had seen that film which had made you so sad.

ANNA. *(Starting to understand.)* Are we feeling a little bit jealous?

HENRI. I will always treasure that night. My "education sentimentale." And no one has to know.

ANNA. *(Playing along now.)* Please, Henri, I thought we had agreed to forget all about it. It was late, you were crying, I was weak for a moment and —

HENRI. And little Emma was made?

ANNA. No!!! That's impossible.

HENRI. But who will Peter believe if I tell him I am the father?

ANNA. Are you threatening me? Are you daring to — listen, I can send you home to Paris so fast it will make that little froggy head of yours swim —

HENRI. Fine. I go home to Paree, the culture capital of the world. I leave New York and its dirt behind. *Au revoir.* No regrets. *Je ne regret rien.* And you? Do you think Peter will leave the baby alone with you?

ANNA. Henri listen, honey — do you remember that night? When you cried against my shoulder and I brushed your hair? You were lonely, you missed Paris, you missed your friends the balloons — do you remember? And you begged me, and against my better judgment, I gave in. Do you remember what I said as I unbuttoned my blouse? "Years from now, when you speak of this — and you will — be kind." *(Pause.)* Now I ask you. Is this kind?

HENRI. *(Quiet, miserable.)* No.

ANNA. Come here, baby. I'd ask you to sit on my lap, but it's a little difficult right now.

HENRI. I'm a big boy.

ANNA. That's right, you are. *(With difficulty.)* Listen — I can't undo what happened to Orphan. But I have never broken a promise to you, have I? Have I? And I promise you that nothing will … hurt you. Or … Cecil. You're my … treasure. And nothing ever will, nothing ever could, replace you. Okay? *(Pause.)* What can I do to make it up to you? Is there anything I can do to make you feel better? To cheer you up? To make you stop this, this silly talk of accidents and patrimony? Hmm?

HENRI. Well … there is a tiny, little something …

ANNA. What can I do? Tell me …

HENRI. Do you remember last year, when you got some money? And at the time, you asked me what I wanted, and I told you —

ANNA. But Henri, baby —

HENRI. And with all that money, what did we get? A movie. Sneakers. Chicken McNuggets ...

ANNA. But you like Chicken Mc —

HENRI. I told you what I wanted, and you laughed at me. You laughed at me!

ANNA. Henri! Where are we going to keep a pony in New York! Do you have any idea how much a pony costs? It's out of the question —

HENRI. I really, really want a pony.

ANNA. I'll think about it. I have to ... talk to Ruth about this.

HENRI. And I'll never, ever ask for anything again in my whole life. You could buy it for me with the money for college —

ANNA. You're pushing your luck. I said I'll think about it. Now, I want your hands washed, your teeth brushed and the lights out.

HENRI. *(Suddenly cheerful and obedient.)* All right. I love you, Anna. Good night.

ANNA. Good night. *(Henri goes to the bedroom door and stops, suddenly overcome with doubt and fear.)*

HENRI. Anna?

ANNA. What is it now?

HENRI. Do you think maybe I could sleep with you and Ruth just for tonight? *(Anna stares ahead in worry.)*

Scene 11

The next morning. Anna and Ruth sit at the kitchen table.

ANNA. Okay. Here's how I want it to be. Henri's having a relapse, because of Orphan's death. He's seeing balloons again — every time he looks out the window, there they are, a flock of balloons. He's convinced that the balloons have come to take him home to Paris. Before we can stop him, Henri climbs onto the fire escape, and he ... just disappears.

RUTH. Wait a moment — I thought —

ANNA. What did you think?

RUTH. I thought you ... had a change of heart. Last night.

ANNA. I will not be blackmailed. Not by Henri, and not by —

33

(Stops herself.) We've made a deal with Peter.

RUTH. I don't see why we can't change the ... the narrative at this point.

ANNA. We can't stop now. Not in the middle of the story. Don't make this harder on me, Ruthie. *(Ruth is almost to the point of tears.)*

RUTH. *(Angry and sullen.)* Fine. Fine. Just don't make me be here when Cecil has to go.

ANNA. Okay, sweetie. I'm sorry. Let's get this over with. *(Beat.)* Okay?

RUTH. Okay. How are we ... what do you want Henri to do?

ANNA. He goes out on the fire escape, and before we can stop him —

RUTH. You mean he jumps?

ANNA. No! I don't want him hurt. The balloons come and take him away. He just ... disappears. All right?

RUTH. All right. *(Anna struggles for a quiet second with herself. Sighs.)*

ANNA. Henri? Henri, honey, would you come in here? *(Ruth changes into Henri without a moment of hesitation. Henri is falsely cheerful.)*

HENRI. Hi, Anniah.

ANNA. What d'ya been up to, honey?

HENRI. Nothing. Just ... thinking.

ANNA. Thinking about Orphan? *(Henri says nothing.)* Henri, honey, you've had a major upset. We've all had a major upset. There's no rhyme or reason for these things. Death occurs by ... chance. But it doesn't mean that anything will happen to you ... necessarily.

HENRI. "Do not ask for whom the bell tolls." *(Henri looks out the window.)*

ANNA. Listen, little man, it's late. Isn't it time you got dressed? I mean, how can we do things together with you still in your cowboy pajamas? Wouldn't you feel better if I got you a clean T-shirt? Hmm? And we'll all go out and do something together? We could go to the park — would you like that? *(Henri furtively glances out the window.)*

HENRI. I ... I do not want to go out.

ANNA. Why? Nothing will hurt you. You're with us. *(Henri looks out the window.)*

HENRI. Grown-ups do not know everything.

ANNA. No, we don't.

HENRI. You could not help Orphanne, could you? Could you?!

ANNA.   No. *(Pause.)* Henri, why do you keep looking out the window?

HENRI.   What?

ANNA.   What do you see outside the window?

HENRI.   *(Eyes downcast.)* I ... I don't see nothing.

ANNA.   The balloons are back, aren't they? You're seeing the balloons again.

HENRI.   I ... I don't see nothing. *(Pause; then:)* My balloons!!!

ANNA.   Where?

HENRI.   They're waiting for me — outside the window — don't you see them?

ANNA.   Henri, there's nothing there. Now I want you to listen to me. You're having a relapse. We're going to see Dr. Weinstein. You're going to get dressed, and then we're all going uptown to see her. Okay?

HENRI.   You must believe me!

ANNA.   Honey, I do believe that you see balloons. But I also know there's nothing there. Once, when you were a tiny little boy, you must have seen a movie —

HENRI.   *La Balloon Rouge* —

ANNA.   Yes, baby, that's the one. And it was a movie about a little boy in Paris who had a red balloon for a friend —

HENRI.   It wasn't a movie!

ANNA.   Then one day, bullies came and popped the red balloon. And as it died, the little boy wept, and balloons from all over Paris came to him, lifted him up and carried him into the sky. And then the movie ended. It was a beautiful movie.

HENRI.   It wasn't a movie! It was my life!

ANNA.   Henri, you think it was your life. But with the help of Dr. Weinstein, the balloons went away. Isn't that right?

HENRI.   My balloons left me ...

ANNA.   You got well.

HENRI.   *(Excited.)* But now they've come back!

ANNA.   Henri —

HENRI.   They've come back for me!!!

ANNA.   You're going to get dressed. Ruth will help you. Then we're going uptown to see Dr. Wein —

HENRI.   I have nothing to say to Dr. Weinstein! *Nada! Rien!*

ANNA.   And then after we see her, we have a great deal to do. Don't we have a pony to pick out?

HENRI.   *(Laughs sadly.)* A pony ...

ANNA.   Yes, that's right. A pony! It's got to be just the right pony for my Henri.

HENRI. I don't want a fucking pony.

ANNA. You'll feel differently when you see it, shy and pawing the ground in its own little stall. Yes?

HENRI. Anniah, look, forget what I said about the pony. I don't want it anymore. Let's forget about the whole thing, all right?

ANNA. But Henri, I thought you wanted —

HENRI. *(Frightened.)* I don't want a pony. I don't want nothing. I don't remember nothing. I just want to stay here with you. All right? Just to be your little boy ... I know I've been a bad boy, but don't let anything happen to me, don't let them take me — *(Henri is clutching Anna's neck.)*

ANNA. Henri, what are you talking about? Who's going to take you? You're shaking. Sshhh, calm down. Nothing's going to harm you.

HENRI. I've changed my mind. I don't want to go. I love you, Anna. Please, please let me stay —

ANNA. Wait a minute, Ruth —

HENRI. You could hide me. In the closet. I'll be good. Hide me from Ruth and Peter, they're trying to k —

ANNA. This is not what we agreed — !

HENRI. Ruth is going to kill me. You don't understand. She'll throw me off the fire escape —

ANNA. Ruth, that's not fair —

HENRI. Please, Anna, please, I don't want to die —

ANNA. *(Crying out.)* Ruth! STOP IT! You're hurting him!!! *(There is silence.)* For God's sake, don't hurt him.

RUTH. *(Quiet.)* I'm sorry.

ANNA. *(Upset.)* Just take him out. *(Ruth turns to go.)* — No, wait a minute. *(Anna seizes Ruth's face, kisses it. Nods to Ruth. Ruth goes to the window, raises it and climbs out on the fire escape. There is silence. Anna sits, tense and upset. Ruth comes back in; closes the window. Ruth turns and goes to Anna. Ruth holds out a deflated red balloon.)*

Scene 12

Peter stands in front of the window in the kitchen, searching the sky. Ruth sits, subdued, in a chair behind Peter. Anna holds her hand.

PETER. What if he falls? What if he drops him?

ANNA. That won't happen. They'll hold onto him. *(Ruth looks at Anna; Anna nods. Ruth quietly leaves the room.)*

PETER. All the way to Paris?

ANNA. He'll make it. *(Pause.)*

PETER. Oh, my God, you guys — what are you going to tell Cecil?

CECIL. I hope you'll tell him the truth. *(Peter turns and sees he is alone with Cecil.)*

PETER. No! I don't want to be here when —

CECIL. When what?

PETER. Cecil! You're home early!

CECIL. Yeah. Where's Henri?

PETER. Um, Cecil —

CECIL. Henri! Henri, I'm home — *(Looks into the other room.)* Henri? Hey, where is he? He's not in his room — is he in the bathroom?

PETER. Ahh, I think perhaps Ruth should be here —

CECIL. Ruth left. She said you wanted to speak to me. Alone. *(Peter begins to sweat.)*

PETER. Cecil, I'm counting on you to take this like ... a man.

CECIL. WHERE'S HENRI? What have you done to him?

PETER. Me? I've — the truth is, while he was with Anna and Ruth, he ... disappeared.

CECIL. Disappeared?

PETER. He's gone. We don't know where. He ... he was acting strange, talking about balloons, and then the next minute, he was gone.

CECIL. Gone? *(Laughs wildly.)* Disappeared? Oh, that's rich — that's really good.

PETER. Umm — maybe I should leave you alone now and come

back at a —

CECIL. Nobody leaves this room!

PETER. Cecil, I know what you must be feeling …

CECIL. I suppose he just "floated" into thin air.

PETER. Well, actually, there has been a sighting over the Atlantic by the Coast Guard —

CECIL. I should never have left him alone with the three of you.

PETER. Now wait a minute, Cecil, I have nothing to do with —

CECIL. Oh, yes. "For Brutus is an honourable man." *(Peter is silent.)* It's good. It's really good. I have to hand it to the three of you. No bodies, no trace —

PETER. Look, I didn't want it to happen this way. I never meant to hurt anybody. I thought … that … that the kids should just go away, not be hurt. *(Starts to laugh and splutter.)* I mean, I'm not a … a murderer, for God's sake, I'm just a … a —

CECIL. A father? *(The laugh dies out. Beat.)* How will it happen to me, Uncle Peter? A pillow in the night? Chinese food gone bad? An accidental case of toxic shock?

PETER. Listen, Cecil, how about if we go inside and you lie down. I'll bring you a glass of warm milk —

CECIL. Warm milk? Laced with what? *(Beat.)* You know what I think, Uncle Peter? I think I knew too much. That's why you have to do this. I know how you got that scar on your temple when you were five. I know what happened the night of your senior prom. How you ran over the family cat in the driveway when you picked up your date. How she sobbed, "Fluffy, Fluffy," and you laughed. Or about the time on the Connecticut Turnpike when you —

PETER. I told those things to Anna! In confidence.

CECIL. Yes. But grown-ups forget these things. Children remember. Children know a whole lot more than adults would like. When Medea called her boys into the house, they knew.

PETER. Oh, God.

CECIL. Remember the night after your father walked out? You went to your bedroom, and packed up all of your soldiers and your airplanes and you marched down the street and gave them away to the kids on the block.

PETER. I don't remember telling Anna that.

CECIL. First year in graduate school. After a party. You'd had too much to drink. We have a lot in common, Uncle Peter; Anna modeled me a little bit on you.

PETER. I didn't know that. *(Beat.)* I guess I don't have to tell you that I've been freaking out a little bit.

CECIL. That's putting it mildly, Uncle Peter.

PETER. I've been trying to remember what my own house was like before my father left home. And all I can remember is how we would tiptoe around when Raymond came home, and he would solemnly put his neat tasseled shoes up on the hassock, while Mother brought him a dry martini. *(Pause.)* Shoes with tassels!

CECIL. I don't think anyone drinks dry martinis anymore.

PETER. No. It's not a lot to go on, is it?

CECIL. I don't think Anna and Ruth would want Raymond to father their child.

PETER. I can't say I blame them.

CECIL. They chose you. Just ... just make it up on your own, this father thing, okay, Uncle Peter?

PETER. Yes. Thank you, Cecil. I feel a lot better.

CECIL. *(Sadly.)* I'm glad.

PETER. So ... so now what do we do?

CECIL. The messenger always gets killed in the Greeks.

PETER. Look — do you think maybe we could ... change the ending? *Deus ex machina?* I'd really like it if you could stick around.

CECIL. I don't think so. Not without Henri. *(Tiny pause; a breath.)* It's been a good life. I'm ready to go.

PETER. I'm sorry ... How do you want me to do this? I've never done this before ...

CECIL. "Our Enemies have beat us to the Pit."

PETER. Okay. Wait, wait ... don't tell me ...

CECIL. *Julius Caesar*, Act Five.

PETER. You want to die as the noblest Roman of them all!

CECIL. Yes, I think that would be appropriate to the occasion, don't you? "Hold then my sword, and turn away thy face."

PETER. *(Now totally engaged.)* "Give me your hand first."

CECIL. Hold it steady. *(Peter and Cecil arrange the "sword" a few times so that the angle misses Anna's belly.)* Good. Good man. By the way ... I think you're going to make a wonderful father. *(He "runs" on the "sword." Dying.)* Promise ... me ... *(Peter holds Cecil tightly.)*

PETER. Anything.

CECIL. Don't ... be afraid ... to play with your child. *(Cecil dies. Anna opens her eyes.)*

ANNA. Petey? Are you okay?

Scene 13

The end of a very long day. Peter and Ruth.

PETER. My hands are still shaking. I could barely get the keys out of the door. I feel like every pore in my body has been drained of sweat. My God. I never want to see blood again.

RUTH. Sit down. I'll pour us some vodka.

PETER. Did you ever imagine? Have you ever seen anything like that? It was nothing like that movie they showed us. Before tonight in that delivery room, I though *Aliens* was science fiction. Those things bursting out of people's bodies — it didn't look human! Did it? Look at that!!! Look at how my hands are still shaking — see? I don't know if I'm laughing or crying. Is this how you feel when you get your period?

RUTH. Drink this.

PETER. Have you ever seen that kind of pain? I don't know how women do it —

RUTH. It's all right now. It's over. Try not to think about it. They say you forget the pain.

PETER. I sure as hell won't. Natural childbirth! Natural! Like ... like volcanoes, or tidal waves, or earthquakes —

RUTH. Drink up. *(They sit and down the vodka. Pause.)*

PETER. The apartment is ... so quiet. It's never been so quiet. *(Pause. They listen to the apartment.)*

RUTH. He's got your face.

PETER. Do you really think so?

RUTH. *(Quietly.)* He looks just like you. *(Beat.)* I guess Anna and I really started talking about having a child after our first year together. You know how it is, that first year ... you spend every moment in side glances at your lover, learning this new alphabet — her face, her walk, her gestures ... the way she holds a pen, the way she chews the inside of her cheek in concentration; how her left nostril flares ever so slightly when she's amused — and you feel so ardent, you're in first grade all over again, in love with your teacher — so much in love that you wake early to study this alphabet while she's still asleep, memorizing her face on the pillow ... And I used to imagine that somewhere in

the United States, there must be a pioneer geneticist, a woman in a lab coat we could go to, who would take some DNA from Anna and some DNA from me — and she'd combine us in a petri dish in a little honeymoon culture at just the right temperature — and then this growing synthesis would be transplanted in one of us, and when he or she would emerge, nine months later — the baby would have Anna's eyes winking beneath my eyebrows. But finally I thought — well, I can always see my own face any time I want to in the mirror. But I could see Anna's face at birth, Anna in diapers, a little Anna coming home from school. Or if the baby was born a boy — even better — I'd see his Adam's apple grow beneath her chin, or I'd experience that awkward moment right before puberty, before his voice changes, when I mistake his hello on the phone for hers — Well. I guess I didn't think this all the way through.
PETER. Oh ... Is my face such an awful face? *(Ruth smiles at him.)*
RUTH. No. It's a very sweet face. *(She strokes his face.)* I'm going to have to learn a new alphabet all over again.

Scene 14

In the kitchen, right before supper. Anna is sitting in profile to the audience, nursing Nathan. Peter, with concentration, stands at the stove, stirring away at a large pot. Ruth is setting the table. Although all three are chipper on the surface, there is an underlying depression and sleep deprivation.

ANNA. *(To Nathan.)* Are you through, pumpkin? *(Pause. Softly.)* Nathan? Are you there? Nathan? ... Out like a light.
RUTH. What d'ya put in the milk?
PETER. How would we like our pasta today? *Al dente?*
ANNA. I'm going to put him down.
RUTH. Anna? Did you get the wine?
ANNA. In the fridge.
PETER. We're just about ready. *(Anna puts Nathan into a small bassinet near the table.)*
RUTH. The salad's on the table, already.
ANNA. Wish I could sleep like that. *(The three assemble at the*

41

table; Peter bearing a large pot of pasta Raphael.)

RUTH. Smells wonderful.

PETER. Pass the plates, please.

ANNA. Looks great. What are the green things?

PETER. Artichokes.

RUTH. Yum.

ANNA. So how was your day?

RUTH. Mine? Rushed.

ANNA. What's happening with the car?

RUTH. Well, I practically had to have sex with the mechanic to get him to even lift the hood. I think it's going to be expensive.

PETER. He's not giving a discount after the sex?

RUTH. I wasted two hours waiting to see if he could fix it, and barely made my eleven o'clock. I told him it's the carburetor.

ANNA. No — not the carburetor. The alternator. It's like going to a specialist — you have to come in with the diagnosis.

RUTH. We should have brought it in the beginning. The first time we noticed that burning egg smell. *(They eat. Pause.)*

PETER. And what was your day like, Anna?

ANNA. Do you want wine, Peter?

PETER. No, thanks — I'll stick to water. *(Peter raises his water glass to his lips; pauses. His hand shakes slightly. He does not drink.)*

ANNA. Well, I had a taxing day. The baby slept on and off; he's having some gas, I think.

RUTH. How do you know it's gas?

ANNA. He's smiling at me, all the time.

PETER. Maybe he's happy. Maybe he's dreaming about the womb.

ANNA. No. It's not normal for a baby to smile all the time. It's either gas or mental retardation … It's got to be gas. No more garlic in the food. Let me tell you, I can smell whatever I eat the next day when I change him. *(Peter blanches slightly; clears his throat. He raises the glass of water to his lips, hesitates. Stares at his glass.)* The artichokes kind of remind me of — well, never mind — He's still producing that postmeconium shade of green …

RUTH. Honey, maybe we should change the subject.

PETER. No, I don't mind. This is the life. Nathan dozing in his cradle; Anna talking about the intimate details — a quiet dinner, a new recipe. Just the four of us. *The McNeil-Lehrer Report* at seven. The dishes. The diapers. Most men dream of this. *(The women look at each other. They say nothing. Pause.)*

ANNA. Well, that's all I have to report. It's heaven. I never want

to go back to work. It's going to be a thrill the day he produces something solid. It's getting to be kind of monotonous right now — the same shade. My mother's living room used to be decorated in a similar avocado and beige — remember the sixties and earth tones? *(Peter takes his glass and peers into it. Clears his throat again. He has a slight — a very slight — twitch. Ruth looks at him.)*
RUTH. Is there something in your glass?
PETER. What? Oh, no. It's only ... w-w-water. *(The women look at each other with raised eyebrows.)*
ANNA. So, Petey — how was the office?
PETER. Oh, you know, the same old shit.
RUTH. Did you get the annual report finished on time?
PETER. Yeah ... no thanks to old Handjob.
ANNA. He should give you a raise. How's the new guy working out?
PETER. Fine. Dandy.
RUTH. I thought you said he was an asshole.
ANNA. An MBA from Wharton and he can't find his fly ...
PETER. It's not very interesting to talk about at dinner.
RUTH. What did they think about your marketing idea? *(Peter has raised his glass one more time to his lips.)*
PETER. Oh, you know ... *(This time, instead of drinking, Peter blows bubbles into his glass. The two women wait.)*
ANNA. Petey, we're trying to show an interest and you're not helping.
PETER. Sah-SAH!!!-Sorry. *(Peter begins to flinch. His leg twitches.)*
RUTH. Is there something you're trying to tell us?
PETER. What do you want to know? About the new Xerox machine? Our capital campaign? The percentage of earned income? The rate of overhead and indirect costs I calculated today for FY94–95?
ANNA. What's come over you?
PETER. The projected contributions from the corporate sector for the next two years? Personnel benefits? I'm hot — now I'm cold — now I'm HOT! It itches! All the time! I can't swallow! My mouth's dry! But it foams! My head is burning! Aching! I'm drowning in saliva! SAH-SAH!!! — *(Peter falls from his chair and rolls on the floor.)* Orphan! Revenge! Oorrrppphannnn ...
RUTH. Orphan?!
ANNA. Orphan! What does he ... *(Peter shows the women his arm; whimpers.)*
RUTH. Orphan bit you! Am I right? Is that it? *(Peter howls in the affirmative. The women are wide-eyed.)*
ANNA and RUTH. Rabies!!!

EPILOGUE

In the darkness, the clown light is on. We hear Henri and Orphan, giggling.

HENRI. In his tushy! That's where.
ORPHAN. T-t-tushy!
CECIL. Cut it out, Henri! He does not!
ORPHAN. T-tushy! T-tushy! *(Orphan and Henri giggle.)*
HENRI. There is no pretty way to say it. Derriere, heinie, behind — the doctor gives Uncle Peter shots in his tushy!
CECIL. He does not!
HENRI. He gets it in the same place little baby Nathan does — tushy shots!
CECIL. Shots are usually injected in the gluteus maximus because of the lack of nerve endings.
HENRI. *(Gleeful.)* But it still hurts!
ORPHAN. Yeah!
CECIL. But in the case of hydrophobia — commonly known as rabies — treatment shots must be injected intramuscularly, in the stomach, which is a rather painful process.
HENRI. Tushy! Tushy! *(Uncle Peter pops up from beneath the sheets.)*
PETER. All right, boys, what is it this time?!
CECIL. We were just … joking, Uncle Peter.
HENRI. *(Solicitously and seductively.)* How is your tushy, Uncle Peter?
PETER. My behind is just fine. But yours may not be if you don't settle down. Do you want to wake your brother Nathan up?
ANNA. I happen to know that Uncle Peter is very ticklish on his tushy.
PETER. No!
HENRI. Really?
PETER. No — don't start —
RUTH. *(Interested.)* On his tushy? *(There is a tussling beneath the sheets; voices of all three adults and three children mingle.)*
PETER. *(With increasing panic.)* No — Anna! Stop it! Ruth! Henri! Ruth! No — NOOOOO! *(At the sound of Peter's voice,*

Nathan wakes and cries.)
ALL THREE. Oh, shit.
PETER. I'll take care of it. You just go to sleep like big boys, all right?
ANNA. All right, Uncle Peter.
HENRI. Uncle Peter?
PETER. Yes, Henri?
HENRI. Would it make you feel better if I kiss your behind?
PETER. That's a sweet thought. But no. Sleep tight. *(Peter crosses to the cradle and picks up Nathan and walks into the living room. Ruth walks over to the refrigerator and removes a bottle; begins to heat it up.)*
HENRI. I think what baby Nathan wants is a peanut butter and jelly sandwich.
PETER. Come with Daddy, Nathan. *(Now Anna goes to the changing table.)*
CECIL. Actually, I think a diaper would be appropriate to the occasion.
PETER. Yes, yes, I know. It's a hard life, kid. Yes, it is. *(Nathan quiets.)* That's a good boy. Daddy's boy! Are you Daddy's boy? *(Nathan gurgles. Anna crosses to Peter. Ruth joins them.)*
ANNA. Look at that face! Whose face is that?
RUTH. He's our cutie.
ANNA. Yes, you are.
PETER. Do you know what we do with cuties? We eat them. *(Nathan gurgles again. A spot begins to grow on them; as it grows, we become aware of New York outside of the apartment. The walls become more transparent, and we become aware of the sounds in the street below: New York City at night.)* That's right! Daddy's going to eat Nathan up! … *(Peter makes gobbling noises. Nathan giggles.)* I'm eating you up, yummyyummyyummyyummyyummmm — Nathan's all gone! *(We see Peter, Anna and Ruth cradling Nathan in their apartment — one apartment among hundreds of their neighbors. The lights stream from adjacent windows where other families in privacy keep their own nightly vigils. The play ends as we hear Nathan's giggles and squeals.)*

End of Play

PROPERTY LIST

Cards (ANNA)
Rubber tub with water, towels, baby bottle, diapers, doll
    (RUTH and PETER)
Book (RUTH)
Bread, peanut butter, jelly, knife (HENRI)
Plate, napkin, silk rose in vase (HENRI)
Coffee (ANNA and PETER)
Cigarette (PETER)
Gag, rope (RUTH)
Shopping bag (ANNA)
Shoes, magazines (PETER)
Red balloon (RUTH)
Baby (ANNA)
Pot of pasta (PETER)
Plates, silverware, water glasses (RUTH)
Bottle (RUTH)

SOUND EFFECTS

Nursery music
Crash
Crying baby
Sounds of New York
Baby giggles

NEW PLAYS

★ **RABBIT HOLE by David Lindsay-Abaire.** Winner of the 2007 Pulitzer Prize. Becca and Howie Corbett have everything a couple could want until a life-shattering accident turns their world upside down. "An intensely emotional examination of grief, laced with wit." –*Variety.* "A transcendent and deeply affecting new play." –*Entertainment Weekly.* "Painstakingly beautiful." –*BackStage.* [2M, 3W] ISBN: 978-0-8222-2154-8

★ **DOUBT, A Parable by John Patrick Shanley.** Winner of the 2005 Pulitzer Prize and Tony Award. Sister Aloysius, a Bronx school principal, takes matters into her own hands when she suspects the young Father Flynn of improper relations with one of the male students. "All the elements come invigoratingly together like clockwork." –*Variety.* "Passionate, exquisite, important, engrossing." –*NY Newsday.* [1M, 3W] ISBN: 978-0-8222-2219-4

★ **THE PILLOWMAN by Martin McDonagh.** In an unnamed totalitarian state, an author of horrific children's stories discovers that someone has been making his stories come true. "A blindingly bright black comedy." –*NY Times.* "McDonagh's least forgiving, bravest play." –*Variety.* "Thoroughly startling and genuinely intimidating." –*Chicago Tribune.* [4M, 5 bit parts (2M, 1W, 1 boy, 1 girl)] ISBN: 978-0-8222-2100-5

★ **GREY GARDENS book by Doug Wright, music by Scott Frankel, lyrics by Michael Korie.** The hilarious and heartbreaking story of Big Edie and Little Edie Bouvier Beale, the eccentric aunt and cousin of Jacqueline Kennedy Onassis, once bright names on the social register who became East Hampton's most notorious recluses. "An experience no passionate theatergoer should miss." –*NY Times.* "A unique and unmissable musical." –*Rolling Stone.* [4M, 3W, 2 girls] ISBN: 978-0-8222-2181-4

★ **THE LITTLE DOG LAUGHED by Douglas Carter Beane.** Mitchell Green could make it big as the hot new leading man in Hollywood if Diane, his agent, could just keep him in the closet. "Devastatingly funny." –*NY Times.* "An out-and-out delight." –*NY Daily News.* "Full of wit and wisdom." –*NY Post.* [2M, 2W] ISBN: 978-0-8222-2226-2

★ **SHINING CITY by Conor McPherson.** A guilt-ridden man reaches out to a therapist after seeing the ghost of his recently deceased wife. "Haunting, inspired and glorious." –*NY Times.* "Simply breathtaking and astonishing." –*Time Out.* "A thoughtful, artful, absorbing new drama." –*Star-Ledger.* [3M, 1W] ISBN: 978-0-8222-2187-6

DRAMATISTS PLAY SERVICE, INC.
440 Park Avenue South, New York, NY 10016 212-683-8960 Fax 212-213-1539
postmaster@dramatists.com www.dramatists.com